Project Management

Project Management, Management Tips and Strategies, and How to Control a Team to Complete a Project

Table of Contents

Introduction 1

Chapter 1: Project Management in a Nutshell 2

Chapter 2: Developing a Worthy and Reliable Team 4

Chapter 3: Getting the Most Out of Your Team 8

Chapter 4: Starting a Project 12

Chapter 5: The Art of Scheduling 14

Chapter 6: Managing Scope and Expectations 16

Chapter 7: Establishing Multiple Levels of Support 19

Chapter 8: The Importance of Consistent Communication .. 22

Chapter 9: Managing All Kinds of Change 25

Chapter 10: Reviewing the Project 35

Conclusion 42

Introduction

I want to thank you and congratulate you for taking the time to read this book: *"Project Management: Project Management, Management Tips and Strategies, and How to Control a Team to Complete a Project"*.

This book covers the topic of project management, and will teach you how to successfully manage a team with the aim of completing a project.

Anyone who works in a management position will likely have to manage a variety of projects of different sizes, durations, and difficulties throughout their career. Effective project management is a skill however that very few people seem to truly master.

This book aims to provide you with practical information regarding what a project manager is expected to do, how they should plan their project, structure it, review it, and ensure that it is a success.

Included are several different strategies for continually checking the progress of your project, managing team members, and resolving conflicts. All of these areas are crucial for successful project management.

At the completion of this book you will have a good understanding of project management, and will be armed with an array of skills and strategies for successfully managing a project of any size, duration, or difficulty!

Once again, thanks for picking up this book, I hope you find it to be helpful!

Chapter 1:
Project Management in a Nutshell

Project management is a commonly used phrase across industries. It is a process of organizing the tasks involved in a project and effectively implementing any changes within a company. There are plenty of organizations that work on projects that contribute to their core objectives and this is how they achieve their overall goals.

The thing about most projects is that they are finite which means that there is a start and completion date for each one. There are specific tasks involved and a specific number of people with distinct skills employed under each project. Fixed budgets and strict deadlines are always present as well. There is a project manager responsible for overseeing each project ensuring that deliverables are made available in a timely manner. They monitor progress, detect problems, and address these urgently.

Regardless of your profession and current role, surely you will be entrusted to handle a project or two in the span of your career, and this is why it is important to at least start understanding the basics of project management. Over time, honed skills in this department will pay off as you will be helping organizations meet their objectives by ensuring that these projects are done on time. On the other hand, you will be helping your colleagues by reducing the stresses that come with the work that they will be doing. As you properly manage, delegate, and monitor tasks, you can help reduce, detect, and solve costly issues as they arise.

The process of product management follows simple steps beginning with project conception. You have to come up with an idea for a project and assess its feasibility. More often than not, the final evaluation will be done by a panel within the organization to see whether or not the project is doable and its demands are realistic, not to mention reasonable.

As soon as the idea gets a go signal, then it's time for project definition and planning. All work needs to be outlined and then each task divided into chunks with expected timelines or schedules applied. Once everything is in place, a team should be created, budgets released, and all important resources obtained. Throughout the project, significant controls and progress checking should be done. Any issues should be detected and addressed immediately. It is always important for the project to be on the right track. After all of the deliverables have been handed to the client, the project should undergo a full review. This enables the company to assess which areas need improvement and which processes are the most efficient and cost-effective.

Aside from varying project types, the processes and approaches used by project managers vary as well. However, the end goal is always the same. It is either to solve a problem or change a process to benefit the organization.

Chapter 2:
Developing a Worthy and Reliable Team

Think about it. You've been given a major project for a high-profile customer and you need to deliver the best possible results and fast. How do you do it? You can start by finding the right people who will help you reach and accomplish the goals of the project in a timely manner.

But how do you go about hiring the right people for your team? This is one of the main obstacles that all project managers face. In some cases, you might have an entire team handed over to you and you simply need to make do with what you have. However, on occasions when you have free reign over selecting which professionals will be joining your team, remember to choose wisely.

The thing about hiring is that it involves both concepts of art and science: 1) art in the form of having clear requirements as to what types of skills you need for certain tasks and so on and so forth; and 2) science in the form of functionality and the ability of your potential candidate to function effectively in a team setting.

Before you interview any potential candidates, you should prepare a resource plan that identifies the tasks involved in the project and the skills that you are looking for. Also indicate the hours of work needed to complete each task and include any machines, tools, or software that you might make use of during the project.

Using this initial list, create roles that have to be filled. This will give you an idea of how many people you'll need on your team. Create a clear and specific job description per role so that you can prevent the overlapping of responsibilities when the work begins. Have clear goals and their respective timelines ready as well.

Do some research on potential scenarios that may arise during the project and make a list of questions around these. Ask potential candidates what they will do should these hypothetical situations arise. It is good to know early on how these professionals think and how well you can rely on them during the course of the project. See who is sensible and who is not.

Of course, prep yourself as well. Do your best to remove any need or inkling to hire someone like yourself. You want your team to be as diverse as possible. When selecting potential members for your team, remember to consider these five key aspects:

1. Start by evaluating each candidate to identify who is the best fit for the roles that you are trying to fill. The things that you have to take into account include a candidate's knowledge or expertise, his/her abilities, and their skills. It is important that most, if not all of these, can be applied to the role in question.

    For example, if you need to fill the role of a bookkeeper, you won't hire someone without adept skills in mathematics.

    But always remember that your decision should not merely be focused on one's skills set. You can always teach or train someone to perform a task effectively. Skills can be learned, but the willingness to accept direction will vary among people.

2. Assess which candidates are best suited to the team that you are trying to build. It is not enough that your potential hires be open and capable of working within a team setting. It is also very important that they are compatible with the people that they are going to be working with.

   Projects take long amounts of time to complete. It is necessary that your team acts all throughout that time like a well-oiled machine, lest internal issues get the best of everyone. Aside from compatibility, it is also important to assess how committed a potential hire will be not only to the team but more so to the project at hand.

   Also take into account people who have open mindsets and different viewpoints as these are the ones who can contribute more to the project, especially when it comes to brainstorming and problem solving sessions. Try your best to avoid those who simply say yes to everything. Always remember that the more ideas that flow in, the better hope there is of achieving something extraordinary.

   Finally, look for people who are results-oriented and are self-starters. Keep in mind that the purpose of having an effective team is so that you need not micro-manage all tasks involved in the project.

3. The more reliable connections you can use, the better. Find professionals who have reliable networks within the company. Good internal influence is always welcome especially when you are dealing with major projects.

   The thing about people who are professionally connected is that they are always exposed to new ideas and knowledge that give them an edge. They know how to get things done in the best possible ways and have the ability to find resources that can help with bumps on the road.

4. Always assess for communication skills. In every team, it is important to have people who actually speak and can talk about things, may it be project developments or issues that need resolving. Good communication is essential to the success of every project. It is necessary to unite a team towards the achievement of a common goal.

5. Probably the most important thing to consider when choosing which people to hire for your team is personality. You want to get people with a positive mindset as they bring new ideas to the table, productively solve problems when they arise, and provide reliable output.

   They take responsibility for their actions and immediately correct their mistakes. They are open to instruction and coaching and rarely express any negative attitudes towards their colleagues. They help foster good working relationships which are needed for the project to be accomplished efficiently.

Chapter 3:
Getting the Most Out of Your Team

Project management is not only about managing tasks that have to be completed but also about managing the people expected to deliver results. For any team to be successful in their endeavor, it is important to have an effective project manager. There are always ways by which you can get the most out of your team. Here are some strategies that you can use to motivate them into being as effective as possible.

A good way to foster motivation within the team is to share business stories every now and then. Business stories can be inspiring, not to mention memorable as they are commonly used to pull customers in. They can be found all over the Internet so take advantage of them.

They are effective with consumers, but they also work well in pulling workers in and connecting them to the company. Employees who feel a strong sense of connection to the company will perform better than those who treat it simply as something that helps them pay the bills. It would be best if you can link these business stories to the actual mission and vision of your company. Make it a point to show them that what they are doing has a purpose. It is also a good idea to show them how their individual contributions matter.

The more specific you are, the more responsive your team will be. Link the company to the story, then to the project, and then to the team members. It is very important for you to establish grounds on why the project matters, and why it is a worthy investment of everyone's time and effort. Share the potential benefits of the project that are not only accessible to the company or to the team, but also to those outside the organization.

It is never a bad idea to set targets - so do so. Don't think about it as putting stress on your team. On the contrary, it helps reduce stress by providing direction for all aspects of the project. With targets in place, your team can better manage their time and plan their courses of action. Defining goals can be extremely useful as it also motivates people and helps foster good performances from everyone.

Give direction and set goals, but keep everything balanced. Keep your expectations as reasonable as possible. You should not force people to act against their capacities. This is why it is important that you be mindful of the personalities and work ethics of the people in your team early on. You should not force someone creative to think inside of the box for example. Put every member in a role where they will perform to the best of their abilities.

As a project manager, you should know that things are not always as simple as they may seem. Yes, you have assessed the abilities of each member of the team and you are ensuring that each member stays motivated throughout the course of the project and even after results have been delivered. However, you also have to understand the value that sufficient training provides.

Part of assessing your team's capabilities involves assessing not only their strengths but their weaknesses as well. As all responsibilities are learning experiences and opportunities for the members of your team to grow, you should see to it that they can learn from their duties one way or another. Provide appropriate training as often as you can so that your team members can hone their skills and get out of their comfort zones.

Always offer opportunities for growth. This will encourage your team members to really invest in what they are doing as they will be benefiting from it professionally. If you see someone with the capacity to perform a task not really in line with his or her expertise, give it a shot by offering them the chance to try it out. If someone offers a viable idea for a project, test it out.

You will encounter bumps along the road and this can be expected for all kinds of projects, big or small. This is why empowerment is essential. Boost your team members' morale and keep their spirits up despite shortcomings. Offer viable solutions for improvement and guide them through it all. Welcome contributions and always respect each other's opinions.

Always make every member of the team feel safe. There may be hurdles, challenges, task changes, and other risks. Be prepared for them and understand that they could happen. Be supportive of the people you are working with even when they make mistakes. Instead of focusing on the negative elements of the situation, think about ways by which you can correct them. Work together to achieve a good outcome, a quick fix. Your focus should be to reduce the onset of problems, detect them early on, and make sure that everything is well under control.

Stay connected. Communicate. Set regular pick-up meetings if necessary or discuss a thing or two while in line for lunch. Always communicate information about the project with a sense of urgency. It is a good thing that everyone is mobile these days. You can easily send a quick message over the phone. Different chat and video platforms are also available; you can use these to always have a link with the team. They may be in different locations but you will always have access to one another.

Finally, create a sense of camaraderie. A strong team spirit is always better than having egos battling each other out while you are trying to finish important work. Be transparent but instill a sense of responsibility within the team. Show that each member has a purpose and are all there to deliver the kind of results that no one can provide on his or her own.

Chapter 4:
Starting a Project

There are different tools that you can use to manage projects better and these have originated from various management frameworks. Like other business solutions, it is always best to have an understanding of what's available and put to use those that are most dependable given your targets, abilities, and general approach.

It is important that you look at a number of different factors when you set up a new project. Examples of these include project objectives, budget allocations, risks, and benefits. You need a foundation for your project and these will help you to establish one. It is necessary to have reason and purpose for whatever project you start because it will require finances, time, and of course, valuable manpower.

Start by creating what is called a business case. This is a document that will help you present the project and its components in such a way that can be reviewed for approval and funding. This is the main deliverable for most formal projects. Most of the time, this is reviewed by the senior managers before it gets sent to the higher offices, if necessary. Without it, it will be a challenge to secure the necessary funding not to mention go signal for a project.

Aside from detailing how the project will benefit the company, you also have to indicate how you plan on achieving the tasks involved, how much the activities will cost, and how long it will take you to accomplish whatever needs accomplishing.

Supplement your business case with a probability chart. Another term used to refer to this is the risk impact chart.

Basically, it helps you determine the risks that you might encounter during the project, estimated timelines of their occurrence, how likely they are to occur, and how grave their effects can be on the project itself.

Risk management is something that cannot be absent from organizations these days. There is always a need to calculate risk effectively so that companies will know if taking on a project will be beneficial or disadvantageous to their operations. It is important to understand the risks involved so that the tasks involved in a project can be executed in the best possible manner.

It is the job of the project manager to be aware of these risks. He or she should also have the capacity to provide ample solutions when the need arises. It does not mean that you should address all risks that come with the project. You should put your focus on addressing those which can lead the company to incur unnecessarily large costs. Just like other things, prioritization is important when assessing and addressing risks. With this chart, you will know which risks to address and which to forego.

You also need what is called a project charter. Aside from indicating the project's purpose, it serves to identify the responsibilities of each team member. The project charter is part of the implementation of the business case that has been approved by senior management. With team members having different sets of skills, expertise, and tasks to complete, you need to establish a sense of clarity and understanding of what the project requires from each one of them.

Chapter 5:
The Art of Scheduling

A project is something that comes with multiple tasks and the need to handle multiple team members. As the project manager, you need to be as effective and efficient as possible when juggling all of these components. This is where the art of scheduling enters the picture.

When you apply proper scheduling, you can plan each task accordingly and complete them in a timely manner. There are different ways by which you can schedule tasks and monitor the people in charge of them. One of the tools that you can use is an action plan.

The action plan serves to detail the approach or direction that you plan on taking to bring a project into fruition. It is best used on smaller, less complex projects though. It helps you monitor all tasks so that nothing is forgotten.

It can include menial tasks such as checking emails and sending out responses, generating presentations for management, or even working on client requests. Aside from the main tasks involved in a project, the action plan should also include a list of the team's daily activities.

Action plans are lists but they are not the same as To-Do lists. The latter focuses on the achievement of one goal while an action plan focuses on the completion of an entire project. With a framework in place, it will be easier for you to complete a project efficiently by finishing tasks in a sensible order. As each task is clearly laid out on the chart, you prevent making costly mistakes and reduce the possibility of any key steps being missed. It will also help you with delegation.

Another scheduling tool that can be extremely helpful is gap analysis. It is quite similar to the action plan but is more focused on helping you identify the processes you need to take in order to complete a task. For the major tasks listed on your action plan, think of several approaches that can be taken to accomplish them. From this list of approaches, you can assess which one provides the best solution. The reason it is called gap analysis is because it helps you identify where gaps, unfinished tasks, exist in your action plan. To accomplish the project, you need to close each gap.

And then there are Gantt charts, which are best used when scheduling tasks for projects of a larger scale. Having a Gantt chart can help you accomplish tasks much more efficiently despite the heavier demands or requirements.

For you to be able to successfully complete a project, you should see to it that you are able to control a large number of activities and that they are completed on time. Any missed deadline can have a domino effect on the other tasks on your list and lead to costly mistakes.

Gantt charts provide a visual of everything that needs to be done including the timeframe allotted for each and every task involved in the project. One look is all it will take for you to see what has been accomplished, what needs your attention, and how much your team has progressed over time.

Chapter 6:
Managing Scope and Expectations

As a project manager, you should be cautious and prepared as things can easily spiral out of control. Even if you already have a number of tasks to complete, more requirements can be added to your plate as you progress. This is why scope management is an integral part of the process. It is an important skill that you should perfect in the soonest possible time. The ability to manage expectations will help you maintain focus throughout the project.

There are different tools that you can take advantage of when it comes to this. The first one is business requirements analysis. Basically, it helps you identify the work that must be done and the deliverables that must be presented to senior management at certain points throughout the course of the project.

Keep in mind that for every new product, activity, or project, there is an underlying business need that must be fulfilled. Even if there is a clear purpose as to why a process is undertaken or a product developed, mismatches between end goals and action plans almost always enter the picture. You might have started off focused with your eye on the prize but somewhere along the line, you might get sidetracked into doing something irrelevant.

It is common among organizations to have client complaints every now and then when what was promised is not what was delivered. In some cases, what was agreed upon is suddenly changed in the middle of the production process. There are also some cases where conflicting requirements cause problems and stir controversy. Most of the time, if not always, new requirements are demanded of you just as you were about to finish your task.

These are only some of the problems that you can easily avoid when you have a focused, not to mention detailed, business requirements analysis in your hands. This process includes discovering, defining, analyzing, and of course, documenting the requirements that a certain project calls for in the hopes of achieving a distinct goal. It helps you define the scope of your project and what has to be done, so that you can properly allot time to each task that might fall under the project's umbrella. It will also give you a clear idea as to what resources you need to have access to in order for you to be successful in your attempt.

If you are able to define a goal, you will have a greater chance of getting what you want. This is highly possible given that you have a better understanding of your specific business needs. The more you comprehend the situation, the easier it will be for you to break down each one of these needs into requirements or tasks that are more detailed or highly specific. It is also easier to address problems given these smaller chunks.

You can also rely on a method called MoSCoW. Developed in the mid-90s by Dai Clegg, it stands for:

- Must – Critical requirements for the project's success

- Should – High-priority but time-flexible requirements needed for the project's success

- Could – Tasks that only need to be addressed if time and resources permit

- Would – Tasks that will not have a grave effect on the project's outcome even if completely ignored

The MoSCoW method is commonly used to sort project tasks under 2 categories; critical and non-critical. It helps project managers sift through the tasks involved in the project that they are handling. Given that you will not have all the time and resources in the world to go over each task, MoSCow helps you prioritize tasks, giving you the luxury of delegating or completely letting go of those which you deem to be minimally important.

By setting a fixed project scope, you can accommodate minor changes here and there but refrain from making too many alterations in the project that can easily disrupt your process.

Chapter 7:
Establishing Multiple Levels of Support

All projects require a certain amount of support both morally and financially. It is important for you to be able to build enough support for the project that you are handling. You may require backing and you should not only think about getting the support of your boss, but also stakeholders, clients, colleagues, and suppliers as well. This is why you have to place a significant amount of effort into pitching the idea.

If you are working in an organization where there are participating stakeholders, you should conduct what is called a stakeholder analysis. This is so that you will be able to identify who the key people are, technically those you need to impress, and know how best to communicate with them.

The good thing about stakeholders is because of their investment in the company's operations, they won't wish you to fail. Not only can you get them to help you shape the project, but you can also get their input and use this to your and the project's advantage. Once you gain their support, you will also have a better chance of gaining more access to a variety of resources.

It is important that the stakeholders understand your purpose, what you are doing, and how you plan on achieving desirable results in your endeavor. If they understand your process, they will be in a better position to assist you should you require their help.

Another good tool to use to maintain a reliable support system during the course of the project is the responsibility assignment matrix. This matrix will help you plot out the tasks involved in the project and the people responsible for each one of them. Since it will surely take tons of effort to maintain control over a project to ensure that it runs as smoothly as possible, you should be mindful of what your deliverables are and to whom you've delegated these important responsibilities. You should know what is happening and how your team members are progressing.

The absence of clarity with regard to work roles can lead to costly mistakes that can cause the project to fail. This is why you should prevent such issues from penetrating your process. Aside from you, the project manager, it is also important that every member of the team knows what is expected of them and what is expected of their colleagues. Things will run smoothly if everyone is aware of each other's responsibilities. Aside from knowing who to ask about certain things, it also eliminates conflict in the form of overlapping duties.

As the project manager, you should know that a responsibility assignment matrix holds value as it is a very reliable tool that managers use to establish and maintain clear boundaries when it comes to the tasks assigned per member of their team. For every task involved in the project, the matrix shows what needs to be accomplished and who will be responsible for this contribution. Another type of matrix that you can apply to your project comes in the form of influence maps.

A project requires ample support and there are different individuals that can have influence over the one that you are handling. Some of these people are quite easy to spot while recognizing others calls for a bit more effort. It is important that you discover and manage these influencers to have a better chance of achieving a highly desirable outcome for your project.

Understand who has influence over your project both from the inside and from outside your organization. Find ways to discover their interests and their objectives in the project, as well as their level of commitment to its needs. Figure out their direction, their nature, and of course, their strengths.

Influence mapping is not only about figuring out who the stakeholders are but discovering the project's true set of supporters. As you find more of the right people, you can influence relationships that can lead you to a successful outcome for your goal.

Chapter 8:
The Importance of Consistent Communication

Communication is an essential part of life and it is a very important element of business as well. When we communicate with one another, we open the doors to collaboration and welcome various ideas and opportunities for growth. When it comes to any kind of project, no matter how simple or how complex it is, there is a constant need for good communication.

Even if you share an office building, there are times when all members of the team won't be in one place as they have other responsibilities to take care of. Even if face to face conversation is what you are interested in, there are times when you have to compromise. It is a good thing that there are different tools that you can utilize for such a purpose.

A simple tool that you can use to track which tasks have been completed and which ones are next in line is a project dashboard. Accessible to all team members, the dashboard ensures that everyone is aware of the status of the project. As the project manager, it is important that you know the ins and outs of the project. No matter how busy you are, you need to have control over things.

Do not expect to have enough time to read through highly-detailed status reports covering the tasks involved in your project. Don't beat yourself up about it as this is almost always impossible. It is common for managers to get certain pieces of information later than desired and this is why project dashboards came to light; to offer a solution to the age old dilemma of time versus information in the workplace.

When a project dashboard is utilized, the entire team is able to update it as specific tasks are started or completed. They can also indicate task progress and note down problems as they happen and update these when solved. Project managers can check the dashboard at anytime of the day to see how things are going. The accessible information is always correct, up-to-date, and most importantly, immediate.

Project dashboards are often always color coded. Most of the time, red, yellow, and green highlights are used to signify the status of a task. Green means that everything is a-ok while red means that a task is in critical condition and requires the manager's immediate attention. Yellow means that a task is in progress but requires attention although not as immediate as tasks marked in red.

A project dashboard should be as simple as possible so that it is easy to read and navigate through. Aside from the color coding, use three main categories and nothing more. Identify the tasks or deliverables, the person responsible, and the status of the work. Have an area for any comments, notes, or feedback as well.

Together with the project dashboard, you should implement something known as the process of project milestone reporting. Although it is important to know when something starts and when it is completed, it is also important for you to keep track of tasks as they are happening. Establish significant points within the project where team members are expected to provide reports of where they are at the task they are currently addressing.

This will give you time to evaluate their work and make any necessary alterations. By checking on tasks every now and then, you will be reducing the onset of costly and sometimes irreversible problems.

Milestones don't only act as points for evaluation. They also help the team understand the progress they have made; when they started, where they currently stand, and how much more of an effort they need to exert to bring the project to completion. Given this information, they will always be on track with deadlines and such, ensuring that the project itself is always headed in the right direction.

You can also benefit a lot from scrum meetings. A scrum meeting is a quick stand-up meeting rallying all team members and getting quick updates from each one. You can also use this time to talk about the project. Lasting for about 15 minutes at the maximum, scrum meetings ensure that everyone is on the same page. They can also be used to motivate team members during challenging moments.

Chapter 9:
Managing All Kinds of Change

Most companies, especially those which have operated and lasted for many years, are often not open to change. This is always a challenge for managers everywhere. Even if it is in their capacity to effect positive transitions; getting ideas considered and accepted is almost always a hurdle that they need to overcome.

You need to be immensely skilled in order to make something stick, especially something as serious as a wide scale transformation. Part of being a project manager involves developing skills when it comes to change management. Change management includes developing skills that will help you deal effectively with different work barriers. It also involves skills in working with different professionals and implementing new initiatives within the organization.

The first thing that you have to be mindful of is overcoming any cultural barriers to change. It is necessary that you hone your skills in addressing cultural issues that may have a role in slowing down or preventing an upcoming change seen to bring positive effects to the organization.

You might be asking yourself how your organization approaches changes within the system. It is important for you to be aware of current practices so that you don't cross anything that does not need to be crossed. You are going to tread on soft ground, so be careful at all times. If you want to pitch an idea, gather all of the necessary information and find reasons as to why your proposed initiative will and will not work so that you can prepare yourself for whatever questions might get thrown your way.

Always remember that every organization has its own corporate culture. Think of it as the blood flowing through the veins of the company. It is shaped not only by the attitudes of the people working there but the organization's experiences, values, and beliefs. This corporate culture is responsible for the company being able to operate as it does. It does not always lead to positive efforts and outcomes but it is the driving force behind the entire organization that without which the company may cease to exist.

You should understand that any organization that has tried changing tactics and failed will be less receptive to another attempt at transitioning. There is also the attitude of saying that nothing broken needs fixing. It will always be a challenge to effect change but this does not mean that you should set any impulse to do so aside. Especially if you see potential and opportunity in a new strategy, then why let it go to waste?

It is a known fact that cultural barriers can often serve as hurdles or roadblocks when it comes to effecting change. However, there are times when these differences serve as the fuel that drive a successful transformation within an organization. As a manager, you should do ample research and figure out what type of culture performs well in your workplace, and which one will succeed. You can then pattern your efforts to mimic these. Not only will it be easier on your part to establish which direction to take for your projects, but knowing what to promote and what not to focus on will also help you make positive internal changes.

Even the best companies do not have a working culture that is perfect. Flaws always exist at some point. For each organization, the operating culture is unique as it evolves from experience and growth. You can't really set a specific goal or peg to aspire to but you can use the successful cultures displayed by other organizations to discover what it is you should be focusing your attention on. It can be the internal processes, your products, or even your people.

Always remember that change is constant. What matters is the organization's acceptance of change and its willingness to embrace new strategies should these become necessary for further development.

The adage "You can't teach an old dog new tricks" holds more truth these days as more and more organizations, especially those which have been around for decades, refuse to accept change.

The problem is that these days, as shifts become more prominent in society, adaptability is extremely important. There are trends that should be considered and new practices that need to be embraced for businesses to stay relevant and remain competitive in a rapidly changing environment.

All kinds of change, big or small, will never fail to intimidate even the best manager in the organization. There will always be a sense of uneasiness that you have to overcome at some point. The thing about change is that even if it is necessary, delivering it will always be a challenge. Where do you start? What should you do? Who should be involved in effecting change? These are only some of the many questions that you need to ask.

It was during the mid-90s when a man by the name of John Kotter analyzed various organizations to understand what people did to effect positive internal change and his studies led him to develop an 8-step model designed to help managers handle transitional change better.

1. Create Urgency

Always remember that your intention to effect change may not come to fruition unless a majority of, or the entire organization, wants it. This is why you should concentrate on creating a sense of urgency for the changes that you plan on applying.

Instead of focusing your presentation on the increasing market competition or the company's diving performance, establish a conversation, a dialogue, and talk about what is happening in the industry that you are in. You want people to talk about the changes that you are proposing. The noisier it becomes, the greater your chances are of having these proposals considered by upper management.

Make it a point to discuss as many details as you can. Start by talking about the potential threats to the organization and lay out a couple of scenarios showing the effects of these threats should the company fail to address them. It is also a good idea to examine the different opportunities available to the organization. The more options that are available, the better. Also present how these opportunities could be taken advantage of.

It is important for conversations to be as honest and sincere as possible. A good tip to keep people talking, to encourage them to participate, is to offer reasons that are convincing enough to consider and will start them thinking about why your proposal is sound. Make an effort to gain the support of influential people both inside and outside of the company. The stronger your support system, the stronger your argument will become with regard to why change is needed.

When creating a sense of urgency, try your best not to foster an environment of panic as this will cause you more trouble than benefit. Like any other project, you do not want to jump in too fast and get yourself caught up in something that you cannot bounce back from. Do your research and study your options. Prepare well and try not to miss any important nooks and crannies. Act only when you have prepared well enough.

2. Form a Powerful Coalition

The ability to establish a solid support system will help you succeed if you want to propose for an organizational shift. This is where your leadership prowess enters the picture as you make your case and convince people to agree with what you are saying. Change requires someone to take the lead and in this case, you are the leader.

Assess the people in your organization and identify who the influencers are. They need not belong to top management but their decisions should nonetheless hold weight. Aside from their influence, you also want to be supported by those with experiences and expertise in effecting change. Talk to colleagues who are knowledgeable about trends. Speak to those who can give you viable input on whatever it is you plan on proposing.

The most important thing is for you to lead this team of influencers to ensure that they work as one cohesive unit. Any semblance of misunderstanding or disagreement among the members of your team will look bad and lead you towards rejection rather than consideration.

3. Create a Vision for Change

One of the wonderful things about change management is that it fosters idea generation. If you are intent on effecting positive change within your organization – then your mind will go places. Let it wander and collect all of your ideas in a pool. Get ideas from your team and influencers as well.

Do not worry about refining these ideas early on. The more you have to start with the better. Once you have completed the brainstorming phase, it is now time to connect these ideas to the problem you are trying to solve.

Focus on feasible ideas. No matter how amazing something sounds, if it is relatively impossible to apply to the organization, then it is plain useless. Establish your vision and explain it properly to the people involved. Make it simple yet comprehensive. It should be easy to understand so that nothing is lost in translation. Keeping it simple opens the doors to consideration instead of confusion.

Have a process drafted out and pinpoint how each team member will be able to contribute to it given their distinct skill sets. The more invested people are in it, the greater their effort will be and the better your outcome will turn out.

4. Communicate the Vision

Unless you are able to explain everything clearly and actually have people listen to you and understand what it is you are trying to point out, all of your hard work in preparing a proposal for change will go to waste. This is why you cannot remove proper communication from the mix.

Aside from communicating your ideas to your colleagues, you should embody the kind of change that you are trying to achieve. Not having any prior consideration should not stop you from making an effort to change your habits. If the organization notices a positive outcome from these small changes, then you are well on your way to achieving success. As they say, be sure you talk the talk and walk the walk.

Also be as open as possible when it comes to answering questions from the people you work with. The more you can reduce their anxieties in line with the proposal, the better. Make them feel as calm as possible. Reduce any of the negative feedback or impact that your proposal may bring. You can also suggest methods as to how your colleagues can counteract these worries.

5. Remove Obstacles

At some point in your process, you will encounter hurdles. Either people will start providing negative feedback or there will be obstacles in terms of questionable support or delayed approval from upper management. Your next task as the project manager is to address these obstacles and remove them from the equation as soon as you can.

If there is any resistance, identify what might be causing it. If there are delays in assessment, check if upper management is busy with something, or if your proposal has been lost amidst other projects that require their attention. Whatever it is that is blocking your way, take action. If you are dealing with people, then have a dialogue and hear out their concerns. Address these as best as you can.

6. Create Short-Term Wins

Success is the ultimate motivator when it comes to just about anything. When you are trying to effect change, see to it that you give your organization a taste of the kind of success that they can attain should they go forward with your proposal. It is important to consider having short-term wins in your process.

Depending on the kind of change you want applied to the corporate culture, schedule time for quick wins that can be felt not only by your colleagues but more importantly by the upper management and stockholders as well. If they are able to feel the effects of success every now and then, they will be less resistant to change.

You need quick wins within your process because a lengthy lag will only cause critics or negative thinkers to ruin your progress. When you draft an implementation plan, you should create short-term goals or targets. Make sure that these are reasonable so that they will be achievable. As much as possible, ensure that there is as little room for failure as possible.

There will of course at times be a couple of challenges that come with achieving these success pockets, but do encourage your team to push through them. After all, every win will further motivate the people driving change. It is also a good idea to reward those who are able to assist in achieving these small wins.

7. Build on the Change

One of the most important things is to build on the change, which means that project managers should understand that they are going through a process which will take time and ample adjustment.

There are plenty of professionals that end up with failed projects because of their necessity to rush their work. What they do instead of focus on the process is put all of their effort in declaring a quick victory.

Keep in mind that real change needs a strong foundation. Quick wins should not be the primary focus here. It always boils down to the bigger picture. This is the only way to truly succeed in effecting long-term changes within the corporate culture.

For example, if you were tasked to launch a new product, you should not jump in too quickly and release it to the market. You should plan your strategy for advertising, marketing, product development, and the like. There are different windows of opportunity that you can capitalize on that will lead you to succeed in your project. In this case, success will come in the form of consumer support and product referral.

When you experience quick wins, you should assess what led you to succeed and what hurdles you encountered along the way. Use this to improve on your process and continue setting goals as you move along the project's course.

8. Anchor the Changes in Corporate Culture

When you have successfully created a foundation for change, you should then focus your attention on anchoring it down. Do your best to make the changes stick. Work towards making it the core of your company. Remember that corporate culture is responsible for determining how the firm operates so these changes should be reflected in all daily processes or else your efforts will not amount to very much.

It is your responsibility to make a continuous effort in seeing that the changes you are proposing, and the changes that have been applied, are seen in the different aspects of your company. Aside from the effort that comes from you, a significant amount of work should also come from the leaders of the organization.

Always remember that the people that supported you throughout the course of the project should continue providing you with support when the time comes to apply the plan or strategy.

There are little things that you can do to maintain this supply of support. You can talk about progress every now and then and share success stories with regard to the changes being effected into the company culture. Make sure that the old members of the organization and the new hires are well aware of these changes and the positive things that they bring to the table.

It is a known fact that change is tough; this is why you should be careful when it comes to all of your actions. There are plenty of things that can go wrong. It is a good idea to learn from mistakes made by other people to ensure that these mistakes do not occur to you and your organization.

Chapter 10:
Reviewing the Project

Whatever project it is that you decide on handling, whether simple or complex, you are required to go through the process of project improvement and review. This is the time when you should assess the progress of the project, what was done, what went wrong, and all other things. Project managers should do this because it is important for them to continuously improve.

The initial project review is referred to as the 'After Action Review'. This is a process used by project managers to analyze the project's course. Aside from giving the manager an opportunity to make certain adjustments to the strategy in play, this also helps the manager act towards improving the overall performance of the project.

The thing about project reviews is that most of the time, they are conducted when the project has already ended. But it is better for these reviews to be conducted throughout the course of the project, and at specific points of the process, so that the person in charge can make adjustments that can help reduce the onset of costly mistakes. When it comes to the After Action Review, it is conducted after every major task is completed.

If you conduct a review after the project has been completed, it might be too late for you to counteract problems that arose during the process. Surely you will have already used too many resources, not to mention too much time that reverting back to correct a problem area may be close to impossible if not too expensive.

It would definitely be better to evaluate along several milestones. You will learn a lot from this and this knowledge will help you reduce mistakes and better address obstacles that you will face. There are tons of benefits that come with this type of ongoing review.

One of the ways in which an After Action Review can help you is by providing an opportunity to assess the project in terms of what happened and why it happened. Using these details, you can start discussions with the organization that serve to foster learning and understanding. It will open doors for everyone to pitch new ideas as to how things can be done differently to generate an outcome that is more desirable if not more effective.

Depending on how complex the project is, the review may be done after the project is completed or at certain moments during its course. It depends on the organization. The goal of this review remains the same whatever approach the company decides on doing. It exists to help companies find and use the best practices, not to mention innovative approaches, to ensure that they complete tasks efficiently and effectively.

Just as you are evaluating tasks after they have been completed, make it a point to evaluate their effects after implementation as well. The post-implementation review can be used to assess the deliverables of each task to see if all have been provided and to check whether or not additional work or effort will bring about an even better outcome.

When you complete a project, do not think of it as the job being over. The process of project management does not end when a project ends because you still have to monitor its effects and make necessary adjustments along the way. Doing so ensures that the organization benefits from the project's deliverables.

By managing the project long after every strategy has been applied, you are making sure that what you set out to do, all of the goals that you started out with, are actually being achieved. Remember that your project had the goal of delivering a process that addressed the needs of your organization, so make sure that they are able to do so. This is how you can truly say that you have succeeded in this endeavor.

When it comes to the Post-Implementation Review, you should understand that the project that you are handling is not a finite element. This means that even after all of the tasks have been completed, you still have to guard the process and analyze it from time to time.

In the future, similar projects might be entrusted to other members of the organization. When this happens, they will look at what you've done and use your achievements and experiences as a basis for the work that they will be doing. They will use your effort and learn from them in order to achieve something even better for the organization. This ensures that mistakes will occur less and less throughout the process.

For the organization itself, the post-implementation review is of tremendous value. From it, the company can learn how additional benefits can be achieved effectively and efficiently.

One of the things that you should be mindful of when it comes to this is proper timing. Knowing when to conduct your review is very important, as doing it prematurely or too late into the process will not do you any good. The best time to conduct this type of review is within a few weeks after the project deliverables have been provided by the team members. It is during this time that they will have the strongest memory of the processes and steps that they undertook to complete their distinct tasks.

Do not conduct the review right after the project is finished as you still need the changes to take effect. A period of adjustment is necessary for you to review the solution well enough to provide ample feedback. One of the best measures to consider is letting one business cycle pass before you conduct your post-implementation review.

Focus on several elements when you conduct your post-implementation review. Start the process by asking for openness not only from your team members but backers as well. It is necessary that you emphasize the importance of openness and honesty during the assessment. See to it that everyone has a voice and will be heard without repercussion should the feedback be negative in nature.

Listen to people but be as objective as you can. When you engage in a discussion, talk about the processes using objective terms and instead of focusing on shortcomings, put all of your energy towards potential avenues for improvement.

Have a record for everything. Document successful practices and procedures and make the necessary recommendations that can be used to apply these to other projects. Pay attention to the things that might have led to an increase in the risks that come with strategy implementation and try your best to think of ways to avoid these in the future.

Always set your eyes and mind towards the future. Steer clear of any discussion about past mistakes as these can no longer be changed. Now is not the time to nitpick. And of course, focus on the good and the bad. Positive and negative lessons can both be beneficial to the organization's operations.

When you conduct your review, here are some of the things that you should concentrate on. Start with a gap analysis. The essence of a gap analysis was discussed earlier. It helps by reviewing the project charter as it enables you to see how closely the results of the project matches the original objectives set for it during the start.

Do not forget to review the expected deliverables as well. This includes all pertinent documentation. Also see to it that these have been provided in the best possible quality. If not, make sure that an acceptable substitute is provided in its place. If you find any other gaps within the process, find ways to close them. Find potential resolutions that you can apply in the quickest way.

It is also important that you successfully determine which of the project goals have been achieved and which ones have not, if there are any. Assess whether or not the deliverables functioned as was expected. If there are significant error rates, check if the figures are acceptable considering the complexity of your tasks.

Also check on whether or not the achieved strategies are functioning well and if they can be used for future operations within the organization. Also assess all strategy users to see if they have received adequate training and support during the entire process. Without the right training, they will not be able to apply the changes properly and this can cause serious problems over time. You always need people with the right skills for the job.

Establish controls and systems if they haven't been established and make sure that these work perfectly. If there are routine activities that are needed to support the project, check if these exist and identify which ones are crucial to the success of the project. Also, have a ready plan for addressing any issues that may arise in the future.

As part of your review, do not forget to determine the satisfaction of your backers, especially the stakeholders of the company. Analyze if their needs were met and assess the effects of the changes on these people. If you fell short in meeting their desires; try to figure out how you can remedy the situation, and fast!

Analyze the costs as well as the benefits of the project. Measure all final costs and compare them with your initial projections. If you went under budget, figure out where you managed to save money. If you spent more than what was planned, identify which components led to the additional spend. Also measure how much more the benefits of your project outweigh the costs that have been incurred. Are there areas for improvement? If there are, jot these down on your report as well.

Finally, identify which areas can be improved upon, what lessons have been learned throughout the course of the project, and provide your findings and recommendations on a clear copy for everyone involved.

You should review the project to see if all expected benefits have been achieved. If not, what went wrong and how can you address these for future projects? Are there areas that allow for further training or skills improvement? Is it possible to deliver even greater value now or over time? Are there other benefits that can be achieved from this particular project?

Don't only review the process involved or the visible outcome. Focus on reviewing key documentation as well. You have a team so use it to your advantage. Gather all project documents and go over them one by one. If possible, get the help of independent reviewers to remove any biases from your final recommendation report. Make it a point to use appropriate data collection practices to ensure that your supporting data are always in check. Of course, make sure that you deliver appropriate reports as well.

Take all of these in stride and you will be well on your way to becoming an effective, not to mention efficient, project manager. Learn from every task you handle and make sure that you note down the lessons that you attain from each action that you take. As you experience handling more projects, whether simple or complex, you will be able to develop your skills even further and become a stronger asset within your organization.

Conclusion

Thank you again for taking the time to read this book!

I hope this book was able to help you to understand the ins and outs of project management.

The next step is to start honing your skills so that you will become an effective project manager regardless of the complexities of the projects you are assigned to handle.

Finally, if you enjoyed this book, then I'd like to ask you for a favor, would you be kind enough to leave a review for this book on Amazon? It'd be greatly appreciated!

Thank you and good luck!

www.ingramcontent.com/pod-product-compliance
Lightning Source LLC
LaVergne TN
LVHW020446080526
838202LV00055B/5356